My Family to Help People

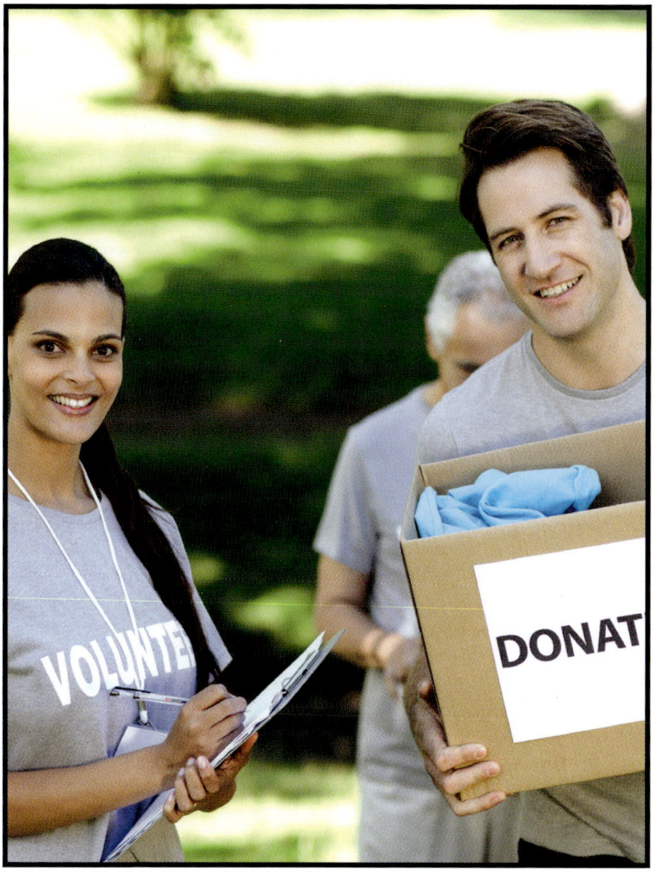

Piper Nelid

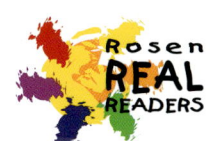

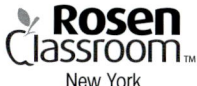

New York

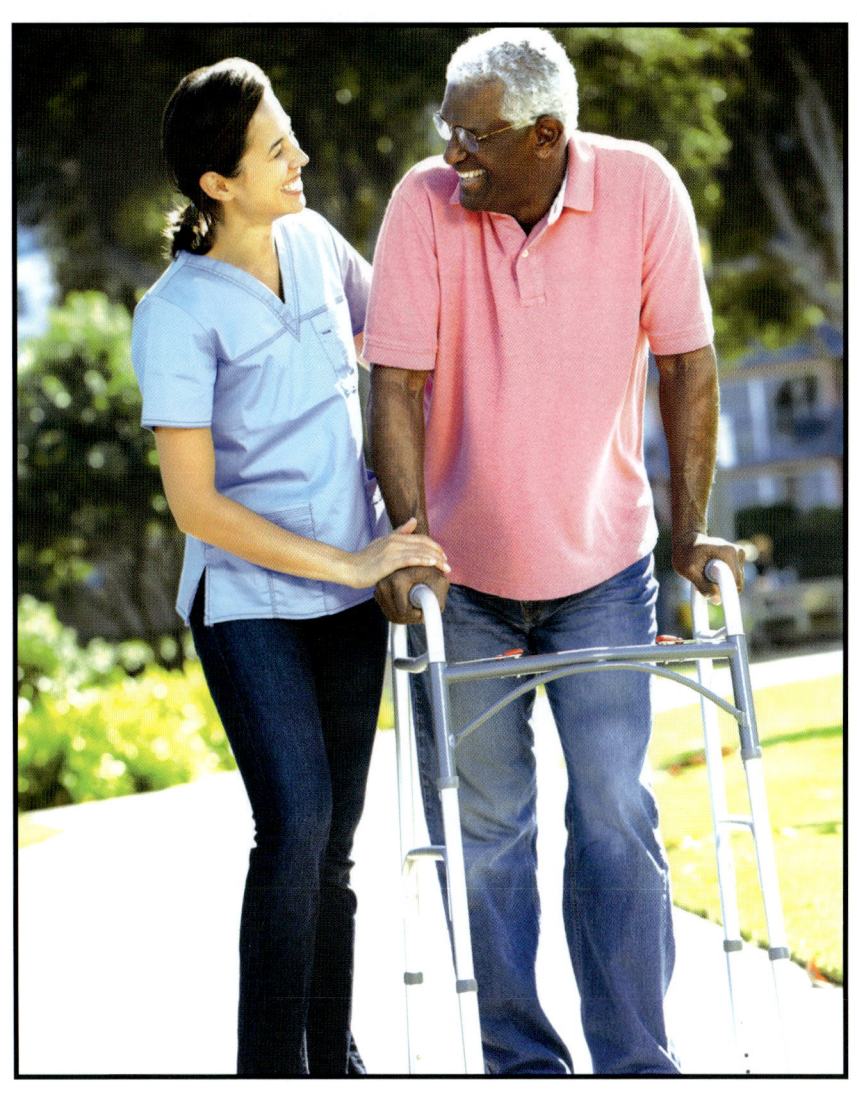

We help older people.

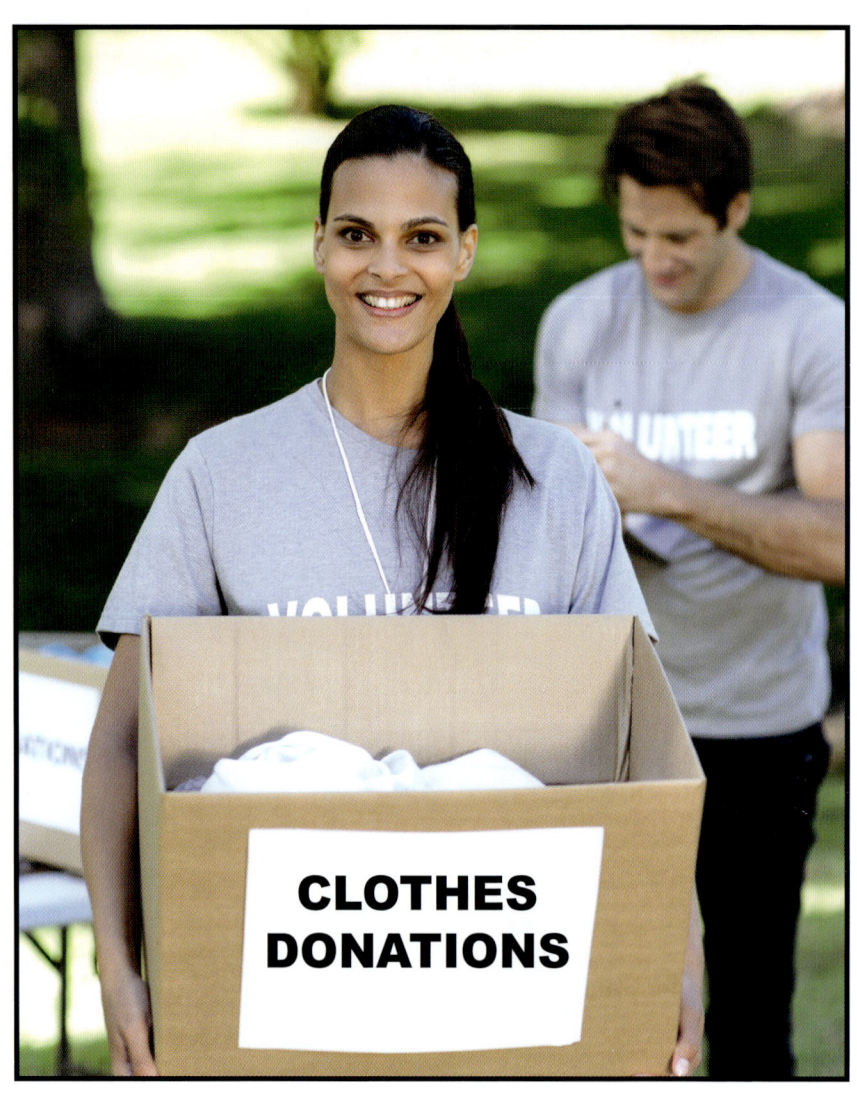

My sister collects clothes to help.

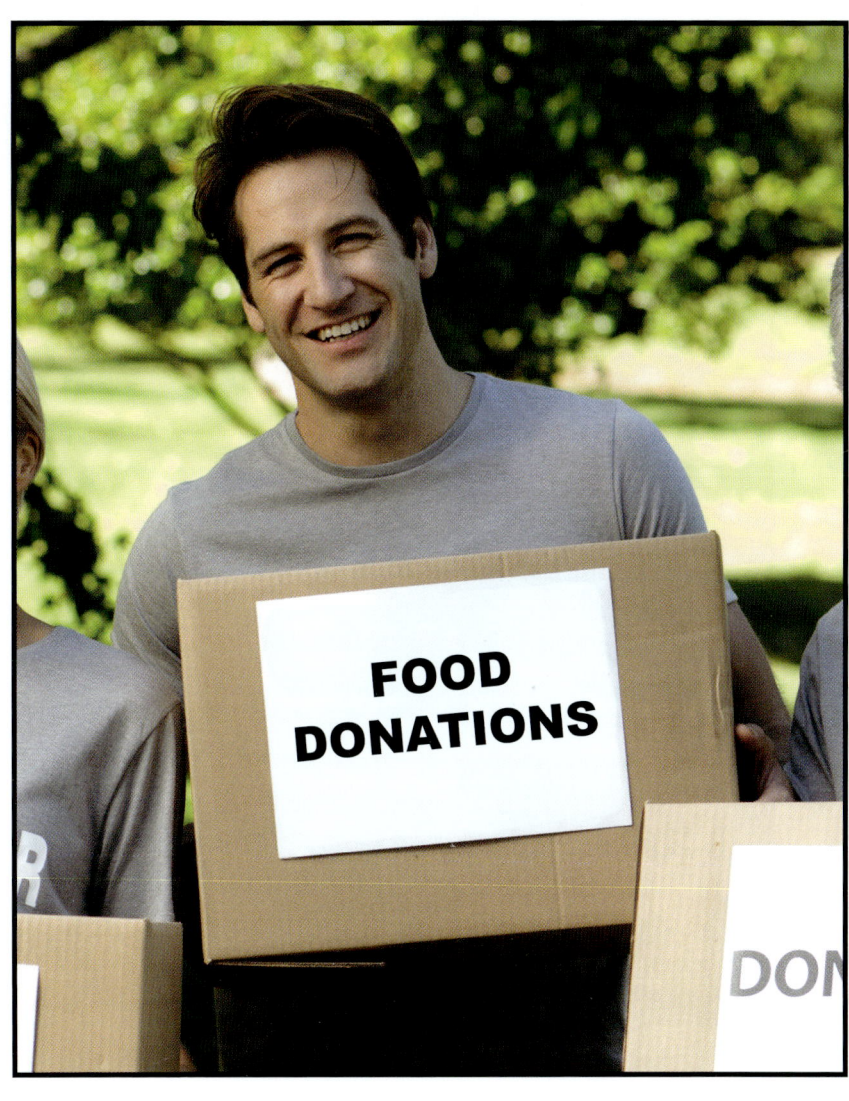

My brother collects food to help.

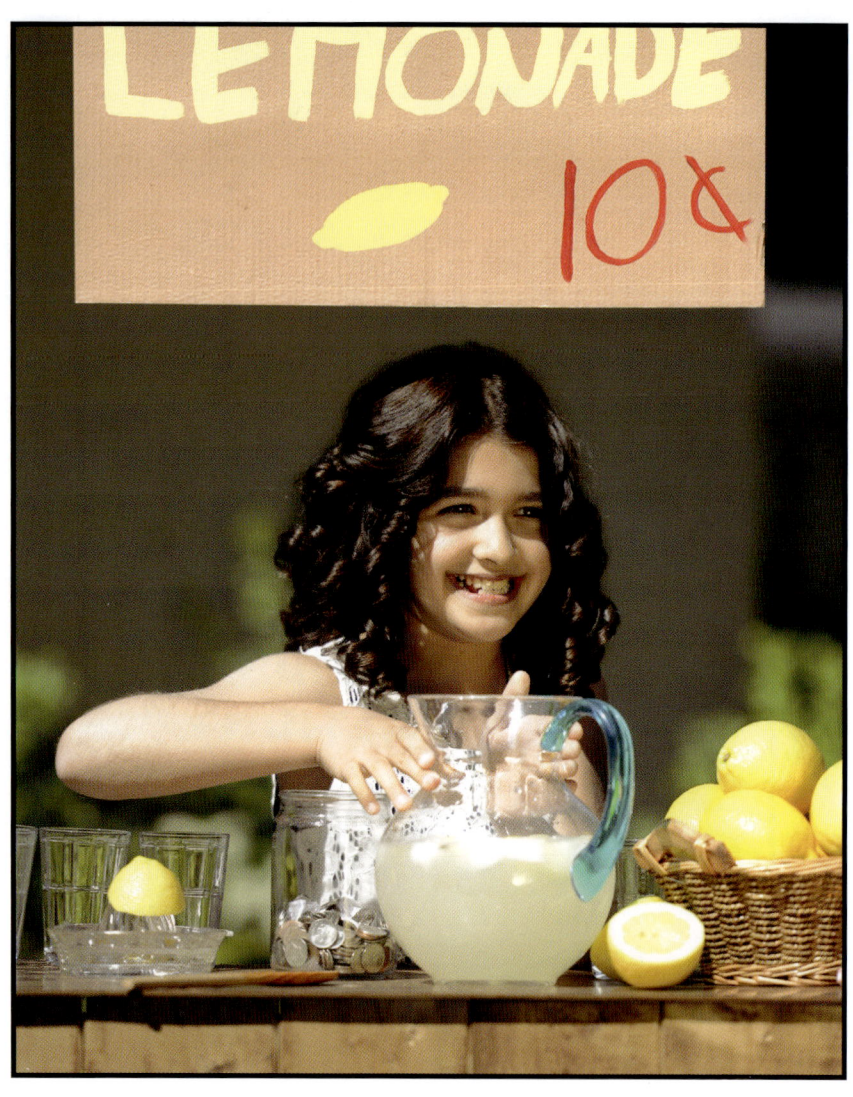

I raise money to help.

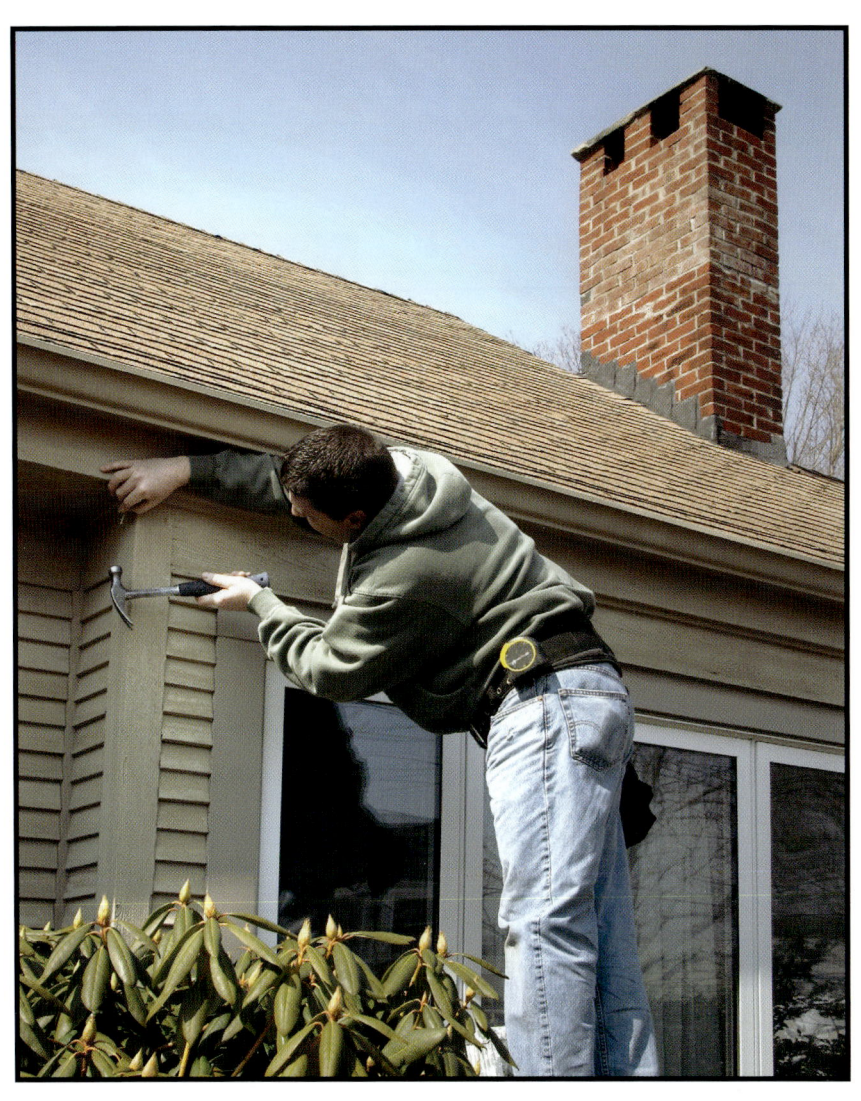

My dad fixes homes to help.

Words To Know

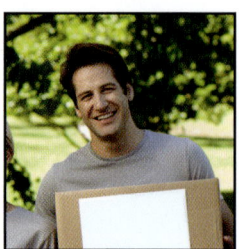
brother

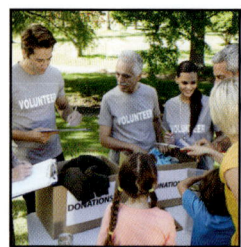
family

money

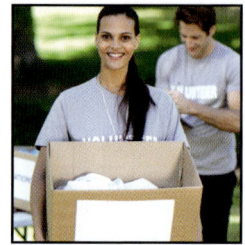
sister